E is for Empathy

Witten by Breanna Lynn
Illustrations by Indira Zuleta

Copyright © 2021 Breanna Lynn

All rights reserved. This book or any portion thereof may not be reproduced or used in any manner whatsoever without the express written permission of the publisher except for the use of brief quotations in a book review.

Published in the United States of America by Breanna's Books.

ISBN 978-1-7366117-1-5 (Hardback)

978-1-7366117-0-8 (Paperback)

E is for Empathy.
It is a simple word, you see.
Spelled E-M-P-A-T-H-Y,
it holds special meaning,
and I will tell you why.

"Em-pa-thy": all one word and easy to say.

Once you show what it means, you could make someone's day.

Empathy means to understand and share the feelings of another.

This can be your mom, your cat, or even your little sister or brother.

When you understand someone else's feelings, you feel like you truly "get it."

You two are on the same page without that person having to say it.

Empathy, empathy, the word of the day.

Empathy can be used in oh-so-many ways.

You can show empathy, be empathetic, or empathize for days.

The best part of empathy is that it is not just for people you know.

You can have empathy for the new kid in class or your favorite character on a TV show.

Empathy is a kind way of showing the world you care. For example, imagine a little girl holding her most favorite teddy bear.

Say you saw the little girl crying because she lost that teddy bear.

Would you feel sad with her? Or would you turn your back and not care?

For those of you that feel sad, what you feel is empathy. You may remember what it feels like to lose something you love a time or two or three.

Even if you have not lost your teddy bear, you can relate to what others feel.

You are being empathetic by showing others their feelings are true and real.

Empathy, a fun word to say and even better to show too.

Let's give an example of how someone can show empathy towards you!

Say you bump your knee and you have to sit out from recess on the playground, and a kid from your class comes to sit by your side and says, "I am sorry that you are down." They are showing empathy because they relate and took some time to come and be around.

Showing empathy can be simple and done in a few quick steps:

Find someone you relate to when their life feels like a mess.

Offer support and show that you care.

Give them that feeling that you will be there.

Showing empathy does not cost a thing.

It just involves being a kind human being.

You can show empathy with ease and care.

Just be honest, open, and willing to share.

You are well on your way to being an **EMPATHY STAR!** You got this. You are ready, and remember to be who you are.

You learned a lot, so let's review:

Empathy is the practice of looking at the world from another's point of view.

Empathy is the action of walking around in another person's shoes.

Remember, when we have more empathy in our world, we simply cannot lose!

Made in United States
North Haven, CT
23 February 2022